WEST HIGHLAND STEAMERS

A PICTORIAL RECORD 1967–2007

THE WEST HIGHLAND STEAMER CLUB

AMBERLEY

First published 2014

Amberley Publishing
The Hill, Stroud
Gloucestershire, GL5 4EP

www.amberley-books.com

British Library Cataloguing in Publication Data.
A catalogue record for this book is available from the British Library.

ISBN 978 1 4456 4417 2 (print)
ISBN 978 1 4456 4430 1 (ebook)

Typesetting and Origination by Amberley Publishing.
Printed in Great Britain.

Introduction

In 1967 a group of like-minded individuals got together to form an organisation dedicated to the appreciation of the vessels of David MacBrayne and the areas of Scotland's glorious West Coast that they served. Out of this initial meeting was born the West Highland Steamer Club. Having started as an informal group that met in a member's house, it soon grew until meetings were being held in a public hall and a formal syllabus was being put together. As well as providing a forum for talking about the vessels and looking at photographs and slides, it also dedicated itself to researching MacBrayne history, both in terms of the ships and of the company and its staff. Out of this grew a newsletter, which was produced twice a year, indicating what each vessel had done in the previous six months together with general background information. This was initially in typewritten format but soon developed into what became known to one and all as 'The Red Book'.

As well as news, this also contained a collection of ship photographs taken during the period under review, portraying both everyday and special events, and the club was most fortunate in having two prominent photographers who supplied the bulk of the illustrations used. In Jim Aikman Smith and Hamish Stewart the club had access to a collection of topical and beautiful photographs that would have graced the pages of any publication.

Jim Aikman Smith (JAS to his friends) was a solicitor by profession and was a native of Edinburgh. From an early age he had been taken on holidays to the West Coast and had quickly fallen in love with the vessels and the landscape. In his early years Jim rather kept himself to himself and did not greatly mix in the society of enthusiasts. Instead, he dedicated himself to building up a network of contacts among the officials of the company, the seagoing staff and those employed on the piers. In so doing he built up a spy network that would have been the envy of the CIA and from whom he received regular information about what was going on and regular tips about upcoming special events. Jim's professional area of experience was in the conveyancing of large estates, and this frequently led him to all parts of the Highlands and Islands. It also gave him the freedom to take off as required upon receiving information about a particular special event. He became a ubiquitous sight all over the Highlands and Islands to such an extent that crews began to look out for him. Captain Robin Hutchison, who was tasked with bringing one of the Humber-built *Loch* car ferries on its delivery voyage to the Clyde, remarked that Jim sprang up literally everywhere from the Humber to the Caledonian Canal. When he didn't appear one morning, they actually waited for him in case he was late! When *Columba* sailed out to St Kilda in May 1978 she spent some time lying in Table Bay. A light aircraft flew overhead and, as one, enthusiasts shouted, 'That will be Jim!'

Jim took a wealth of photographs and, like a true enthusiast, didn't believe in taking one when several would do. He would always appear with several cameras around his neck, and each shot was taken in both colour and black and white. Only those he deemed worthy were ever turned into photographs or slides while the rest languished as negatives. Over the years he built up an amazing collection, which was truly encyclopaedic in nature, and acquired knowledge of the company and its affairs of a similar nature. Such was his knowledge that he was frequently consulted by MacBrayne and CalMac officials as to what duties individual vessels had performed, it being widely held that 'Jim will know'!

When Jim died in 1996 his passing left a void that the club thought would be hard to fill. However, Hamish Stewart of Bearsden volunteered his services and thus provided the club with the services of an excellent photographer. Hamish was a quantity surveyor by profession, latterly in the employ of Renfrewshire Council. Unlike Jim, Hamish came late into the world of the steamer dreamer and initially was interested in the world of aircraft. He seemingly became a weel-kent sight in the environs of Glasgow airport, peering through the perimeter fence to take his shots. Thanks to the good offices of Gordon Law, Hamish was introduced to the land of MacBrayne and quickly became fascinated by the vessels and their environs. With no disrespect intended Hamish was more of a professional at photography than Jim and his views were constructed in such a way as to be works of art. As time permitted Hamish ranged the length and breadth of the West Coast and the Islands, building up a portfolio of exquisite creations. Latterly he particularly specialised in photographs taken in the Oban area, where he and his wife had purchased a flat.

As Robert Burns said, 'The best-laid schemes o' mice an men gang aft agley,' and this could have been aimed particularly at steamer photographers. Many were the plans made that fell apart due to unforeseen circumstances. Jim in particular had more than his fair share of fun and games. He always talked of the day that he tramped for miles over walls, through peat bogs and over a rock face to photograph *King George V* sailing into Loch Creran in Morvern only to be rewarded by the sight of her regally steaming past the entrance, her Master having decided to miss the loch due to late running. When told that, uniquely, the same vessel and *Clansman* were overhauling in adjacent dry docks in Greenock, Jim naturally came through to capture the event. The East India dry docks were notoriously difficult to take such a shot in and so when he espied a building site and a ladder, up he went. While taking his photographs he didn't notice the posse of flashing blue lights gathering on the street below. Unfortunately for Jim, he had decided to climb into the new police headquarters building, and Strathclyde's finest assumed he was a terrorist up to nefarious activities!

Hamish also had his fun. On one occasion he decided that he wanted a shot of *Lochmor* alongside at Canna. The only way to do this was on a Saturday and involved getting her at 0600 on the first of her two Round the Islands voyages, going ashore at Canna to photograph her. He was then to return on *Iona*, which was due on a National Trust cruise on the Sunday. This cruise never reached Canna due to adverse weather conditions, and on returning to the pier, Hamish heard the glad news that he was stranded until Monday! Although he wouldn't have appreciated it at the time, he was actually quite fortunate. A poor BT engineer went out to the Small Isles just before Christmas one year to do an emergency repair and found himself stuck there because of the weather until mid-January!

Sadly, neither Jim nor Hamish lived to the ripe old ages they deserved and both passed away without having been able to enjoy long and active retirements. However, they left us a legacy of excellent photographs that capture the essence of the world of MacBrayne. In the following pictures you will find a selection of their work. That they have been put together in one volume will hopefully serve as an excellent memorial to two wonderful gentlemen.

To widen the range of vessels covered, some photographs taken by other photographers have been included. Each is accompanied by the name of the photographer.

Jim Aikman Smith

Cutting the 25th anniversary birthday cake on board *Isle of Mull*. From left to right: Robin Love, WHSC Treasurer; Jimmy Birse, WHSC Vice-President and CalMac; Gordon Law, WHSC President; Brian Wilson, MP for North Ayrshire; Jim Aikman Smith, WHSC Secretary; and Moira Hirst, a long-standing member of WHSC. A special lunch was held on *Isle of Mull* on Saturday 27 March 1993 to celebrate the club's first twenty-five years.

Lochfyne (1931)
Lochfyne was built to serve as an excursion steamer from Oban in summer and to maintain the Ardrishaig mail service in winter. In 1959 she was transferred to the Clyde service full time and remained as such until 1969. However, in most springs she returned to Oban to provide the early season excursions, her catering facilities being better suited to the party traffic. Here she is photographed in the Sound of Iona on 1 June 1968. (The late Peter G. Herriot)

Lochfyne
For most of her life *Lochfyne* was associated with the Ardrishaig mail service, serving from 1959 on a year-round basis. She is seen arriving at Tarbert ex Ardrishaig on 21 August 1969. In a matter of weeks she would be withdrawn from service and MacBraynes' involvement with the Royal Route would be no more after over 120 years. (Lawrence Macduff)

Lochnevis (1934)
Affectionately known as the 'Moving Spanner', *Lochnevis* found herself at most of the ports and islands served by the company during her lifetime. One route on which she made a regular appearance was the Islay service, where she relieved *Lochiel* for annual overhaul. In addition, from 1965 to 1969, she supplemented that vessel's service to cope with the ever-increasing volume of cars. She is seen alongside at Port Ellen.

Lochnevis
From 1959 until 1969 *Lochnevis* was employed in the summer as the second Oban cruise vessel, partnering *King George V*. In this capacity, she regularly visited Fort William with onward connections to Inverness, Tobermory, Loch Sunart and cruises to the Six Lochs. She is pictured in 1968 arriving at Fort William.

King George V (1926)

Built in 1926 and acquired in 1935, this magnificent vessel became synonymous with cruising out of Oban. Locals always remarked that her appearance heralded the start of summer. Although primarily remembered as the Staffa and Iona vessel, she was also employed on other cruises and is seen passing Glenborradale while sailing up Loch Sunart on 19 May 1969.

King George V
The Sacred Isle cruise to Staffa and Iona rotated on a daily basis between sailing clockwise or anticlockwise around Mull. On each day, one call was made at Tobermory. In this shot she is seen passing Rubha Na Gall lighthouse inbound to Tobermory while sailing in a clockwise direction.

King George V and *Bute*
For the first few months of the 1973 summer season, the Mull ferry service was entrusted to *Bute*, as the designated vessel, *Iona*, was on the Stornoway route because of the late delivery of the rebuilt *Clansman* at Lewis. Meanwhile, as a new end-loading berth was being built at Oban, *King George V* had to berth overnight at Craignure. Thus, on 27 May, the latter is seen berthed at the off-duty berth at Craignure while the former swings in to berth at the ferry berth.

Lochiel (1939)
For just over thirty years, Islay was served by the faithful *Lochiel*. In addition, she also served Colonsay, Gigha and Jura, making one round trip per day to either Port Ellen or Port Askaig. She is seen leaving Craighouse in June 1961.

Loch Seaforth (1947) and *Loch Carron*
Having been superseded at Stornoway by *Iona*, *Loch Seaforth* in turn replaced *Claymore* on the Inner Isles service from Oban in 1972. She is shown on 11 August 1972, passing Rubha Na Gall lighthouse while *Loch Carron* waits to replace her alongside Tobermory pier.

Loch Seaforth
A typical afternoon at Kyle of Lochalsh, September 1968. *Loch Seaforth* is alongside the Railway Pier, loading cargo and passengers for Stornoway, while the CSP's Skye ferry *Coruisk* is leaving, bound for Kyleakin. Note the steam crane in operation at the pier.

Pioneer
In an emergency, on Saturday 3 May 1980, *Pioneer* operated the service from Oban to Coll and Tiree. This also included a call at Tobermory but as the pier was closed, awaiting a decision on its future, the Kilchoan ferry *Lochnell* tendered to her. The small vessel is seen leaving her to return to Tobermory.

Loch Broom (1948)
Originally constructed as the coastal patrol ship *Empire Maysong*, *Lochbroom* joined the fleet in 1948. The company operated a wide range of cargo services and it was said that there wasn't a single building or township on the West Coast that hadn't arrived on a MacBrayne ship! After serving Islay from Glasgow, *Lochbroom* was spare by 1969 and is seen here laid up in Queen's Dock on 27 March of that year. (Lawrence Macduff)

Loch Buie (1949)
In 1949, as part of the 1947 mail contract, a new service was instituted between Tobermory and Mingarry on the Ardnamurchan peninsula. This was done to improve links with the isolated community and to stop the Inner Isles vessel having to divert to make a call. The vessel provided was a former RAF rescue pinnace which was refitted and named *Loch Buie*. She sailed as such until 1968. She is seen at Tobermory in July 1960 in the light blue hull that the ferry boats carried for a few years. (Robin Love)

Loch Dunvegan (1950)
By 1970 the car traffic to and from Tiree was more than the mail ship *Claymore* could cope with. To help out, the cargo vessels were frequently called upon to convey excess cars while their occupants travelled by the conventional ship. *Loch Dunvegan* is shown while so employed, approaching Oban.

Staffa (1950)
A ubiquitous site around the islands for many years, the famous 'Red Boats' were small passenger tenders that were employed where no piers were available. Probably the best-known site of these vessels was Iona, where each summer a small flotilla of them were employed tendering to *King George V* and, latterly, *Columba*. *Staffa* served most of her career at Iona, where she is photographed. She was withdrawn in 1967. (Lawrence Macduff)

Loch Carron (1951)
As well as the mail boats to the various islands, David MacBrayne also operated cargo vessels sailing from Glasgow. These vessels called at a multitude of piers and ferries throughout the Hebrides, some of which were quite obscure. Once such was Loch Skipport in South Uist, a lonely outpost built to serve the local crofters, and *Loch Carron* is seen alongside in the 1950s.

Loch Ard (1955)
Built to operate to the Outer Isles from Glasgow, this handy vessel was eventually transferred to the Glasgow–Islay service. She is photographed alongside Port Askaig on 2 July 1967. In a few years the relentless march of the car ferries would render such vessels obsolete and redundant. (Lawrence Macduff)

Claymore (1955)
The traditional mail steamer *Claymore* was built for the thrice-weekly service from Oban to Tobermory, Coll, Tiree, Castlebay and Lochboisdale. However, by 1972, she was almost exclusively used on summer sailings to Coll and Tiree. Once a week she called at Craignure and Lochaline en route. Here she is shown at Craignure.

Claymore
On several occasions in the 1970s when a large cargo or livestock needed to be carried to or from Lismore, *Claymore* would find herself diverted to make a special call at Achnacloich pier. She is seen alongside in April 1972.

Loch Toscaig (1956)

In July 1955, MacBrayne purchased the fishing boat *Irene Julia* and had her rebuilt. Renamed *Loch Toscaig*, she entered service in July 1956 on a new route from Kyle to Toscaig. This eliminated the need for the Stornoway vessel to call off Applecross. In 1964 she was transferred to the Lismore service, although she also relieved on the Tobermory–Kilchoan service. It is in this latter capacity that she was photographed at Tobermory in April 1972, the photograph being taken from on board *Loch Carron*. (Robin Love)

Loch Arkaig (1960)

In 1959 this former inshore minesweeper was purchased, and was introduced the following year on the Portree service. However, in 1964 she was transferred to the newly established Small Isles service, which, from 1965, was merged with the Portree run. Until her withdrawal in 1979 this robust small vessel faithfully served Eigg, Muck, Rum and Canna and is seen leaving the latter on 9 July 1977.

Loch Arkaig
The diminutive *Loch Arkaig* is illustrated passing Eilean Bhan lighthouse, Kyle of Lochalsh, on 17 March 1975 bound for Raasay and Portree. Today, this picturesque spot is completely dwarfed by the Skye Bridge.

Loch Arkaig and *Bute*
The Mallaig flotilla of the mid-1970s: *Loch Arkaig* is seen leaving the port for the Small Isles while *Bute* is arriving from Armadale. Within several years, both had been replaced by larger vessels.

Loch Eynort
As mentioned above, *Loch Eynort* operated the Armadale service in May 1970 while *Clansman* was on charter to the CSP for the Gourock–Dunoon service. She is seen leaving Armadale. During this period a very restricted car ferry service was maintained several times a day by the Stornoway vessel *Loch Seaforth*.

Loch Eynort (1961)
Purchased by MacBrayne in 1961, *Loch Eynort* finally entered service in 1964 on the Kyle–Raasay–Portree service. She carried so little traffic that the route was combined with the Small Isles service in 1965 and *Loch Eynort* became spare. In May 1970, in the absence of *Clansman* on the Clyde, she operated the Mallaig–Armadale service for passengers only. In addition, on 22 May of that year, she tendered to the veteran *King George V* off Armadale while the latter was on charter to the Highlands and Islands Development Board.

Hebrides (1964)
The three 1964 car ferries *Hebrides*, *Clansman* and *Columba* were registered in Leith rather than Glasgow, as they were owned by the Secretary of State for Scotland and chartered to MacBrayne. Upon the formation of CalMac, they were reregistered in the more usual Glasgow. Appropriately, *Hebrides* is photographed at Leith arriving for annual overhaul on 13 February 1978.

Hebrides (1964)
Of the 1964 MacBrayne car ferries, only *Hebrides* remained on her original service throughout her lifetime. However, she did occasionally deviate and in 1981 served Coll and Tiree for several days while returning from emergency repairs on the Clyde. She is seen leaving Tobermory on the way to the Islands on 4 July.

Clansman
In 1973 this vessel was completely rebuilt as a drive-through ferry to operate the new service between Stornoway and Ullapool. Such was the growth of traffic on the route she had to be replaced the following year by the larger *Suilven*. She was then transferred to the Oban–Craignure service and is seen at Craignure.

Clansman (1964)
The second of the 1964 car ferries was named *Clansman* and was placed on the Mallaig–Armadale service. However, as the winter traffic on this route didn't justify the use of a large car ferry, she became the winter relief vessel. In March 1971, for the first time, she relieved the 'new' Islay ferry *Arran*. As she was too big for West Loch Tarbert, she operated from Oban. She is seen leaving Port Askaig on 6 March.

Columba (1964)

Transport links to the Western Isles were revolutionised in 1964 with the introduction of three purpose-built car ferries. The third of these was *Columba*, which was intended for the Oban–Craignure–Lochaline service. She was also utilised on relief duties and she is pictured, in CalMac days, lying at Tarbert, Harris.

Columba

In 1975, after serving on the original car ferry routes to Craignure and Lochaline and latterly Mallaig–Armadale, *Columba* entered a new phase of her life when she took up the services to Coll and Tiree, Colonsay and in summer to Iona. For the first time Coll and Tiree now had a service whereby cars could be driven on rather than lifted by crane. She is illustrated in June of that year at Coll.

Columba

On 3 May 1975 *Columba* operated a special charter sailing which took her from Mallaig to Kyle of Lochalsh, Portree, Raasay and Loch Kishorn. She is seen alongside at Portree while her passengers enjoyed some time ashore in the Skye capital.

Tobermory Highland Games, 1976

It was long a MacBrayne tradition that special sailings were operated to Tobermory on Games Day to convey passengers to what was one of the most important days in the West Highland calendar. The vessels involved normally lay at the pier for a large part of the day while their passengers attended the events ashore. In this picture *Columba* is alongside the pier having sailed from Oban while *Arran* lies outside her, having brought passengers in from Tiree, Coll and Kilchoan.

Scalpay (1957)

After the withdrawal of the Outer Isles mail service in 1964, a new means of serving the island of Scalpay had to be found. Initially a passenger service was provided from Tarbert (Harris) by the locally owned fishing boat *Catriona*. However, in February 1965 the Ballachulish car ferry *Maid of Glencoe* was purchased and, after adaptation and renaming to *Scalpay*, she opened a new service to the island from Kyles Scalpay. She continued as such until 1971, when she was replaced by the *Lochalsh* from the Kyle–Kyleakin service, a vessel that was actually one year older! (Lawrence Macduff)

Arran (1954)

After the introduction of the 1964 car ferries, the next route designated to be upgraded to a car ferry service was that to Islay. A new vessel was ordered to enter service on it in 1970. However, this vessel was rerouted by the Scottish Transport Group to the busy Gourock–Dunoon service, and MacBrayne were given the pioneer Clyde ferry *Arran* as compensation. Looking resplendent in traditional MacBrayne livery, she is seen arriving at West Loch Tarbert.

Arran and *Lochnell* (1947)

In 1973 *Arran* was converted to stern loading but was replaced on the Islay service a year later by *Pioneer*. Thereafter she became spare, operating on a variety of duties. Here she is seen lying off Mingarry on 22 July 1976 while undertaking a special sailing from Tiree and Coll to Tobermory for the Highland Games. Passengers have been taken out to her from Mingary by *Lochnell*, the Tobermory–Kilchoan ferry.

Arran

When introduced to the Islay service in succession to *Lochiel*, *Arran* operated the same format of timetable, with the exception that she was based overnight at West Loch Tarbert as opposed to the Islay ports. She is photographed unloading at Gigha on 16 September 1970. All agreed that she suited the MacBrayne livery.

Iona (1970)
The new vessel designed for the Islay service but diverted to Dunoon was the *Iona*; while so employed, her little dummy funnel was painted in Caley Yellow. During October and November 1970, she was employed on Sundays carrying freight between Gourock and Brodick and is seen alongside the latter on 15 November.

Iona
Iona finally made it to the Western Isles in 1972 and was initially employed on the Stornoway service, for which her funnel was repainted red. She was replaced by a lengthened *Clansman* in 1973 and was transferred to the Mull route. She is seen coming alongside Oban's North Pier with *Claymore* heading into the bay behind her in July of that year.

Iona

In 1974 *Iona* was transferred to the Oban–Castlebay–Lochboisdale service and had overnight passenger cabins fitted in a new deckhouse behind the wheelhouse. At the same time her engine room uptakes were heightened and turned into real funnels. By 1979 she had finally got to Islay but was also utilised on reliefs. Here, she is seen off Tarbert, Harris, on 15 April 1986.

Iona

The 1970 car ferry is seen alongside Uig while relieving on the Lochmaddy/Tarbert service in April 1986. A new berth and linkspan is being constructed at Uig to accommodate the new ferry *Hebridean Isles*, which entered service on the route on 9 May of that year.

Scalpay (1956)
Upon the withdrawal of the Outer Isles Mail Service in 1964 a new service to Scalpay from Kyles
was introduced with the redundant Ballachulish ferry *Maid of Glencoe*. In December 1971 she was
replaced by the ex Kyle–Kyleakin vessel *Lochalsh*, which was suitably renamed *Scalpay*. She is seen
approaching Tarbert, Harris, on 26 June 1974 on her weekly call for fuel. (Lawrence Macduff)

Bute (1954)
Originally built for service on the Clyde for the CSP, she found herself increasingly on Western
Isles service in the 1970s, ultimately becoming the Mallaig–Armadale ferry. She is photographed
at Iona on 13 August 1978 while engaged in transporting lambs to Oban.

Bute
Her first Hebridean spell of duty occurred late in 1972, when she relieved on the Oban–Craignure–Lochaline service. She is shown alongside at Craignure on 23 December.

Bute
Towards the end of the 1978 season, *Bute* was engaged in special sailings to bring livestock from the islands to Oban, a traditional MacBrayne autumn duty. She is shown alongside at Craighouse, Jura, on 24 September.

Glen Sannox (1957)
Although originally built for Clyde service, later in her life *Glen Sannox* increasingly became a Hebridean ferry, sailing out of Oban and Kennacraig. She is photographed in the Sound of Iona on 16 June 1981 while standing in for *Columba*. On the Iona cruise she was unable to land passengers and merely cruised past.

Glen Sannox
While serving as Mull ferry in early 1979, she made two special Sunday sailings from Oban to Gigha to convey a crane. She is seen alongside Gigha on the second of these sailings on 25 February.

The Cumbrae Flotilla, 1976
With the arrival of the large ferries *Kyleakin* and *Lochalsh* on the Skye crossing in 1971, the smaller ferries found their way to the Clyde for service at Largs and Colintraive. *Coruisk* opened the Cumbrae Slip route in 1972, being supplemented by the *Kyleakin*, renamed *Largs*. The latter is seen here at the slip while *Coruisk* and *Broadford* are behind the pier in May 1976. When the traffic was heavy it wasn't unusual to see three vessels in service operating as a convoy! (Robin Love)

Broadford (1966)
Broadford leaving Kyle of Lochalsh in September 1969. Note the side ramps. In the background, work is underway to build a new slipway to accommodate the larger *Kyleakin* and *Lochalsh*, due to be introduced to the route in 1971. (Robin Love)

Lochalsh (1956)
In 1956, because of the ever-increasing traffic on the Skye crossing, the CSP introduced the new ferry *Lochalsh*. She is seen arriving at Kyle of Lochalsh on 9 July 1968. In 1971 she was transferred to MacBrayne and, renamed *Scalpay*, was introduced to the ferry service to the island of that name. (Lawrence Macduff)

Caledonia
On 27 May 1977 she was chartered to carry a special party from Kyle to the Howard Doris oil platform construction yard in Loch Kishorn. She is shown passing through the Narrows at Kylerhea.

Caledonia (1966)
After a not entirely successful period as Arran ferry, *Caledonia* (ex *Stena Baltica*) was transferred to the Oban–Craignure route in summer from 1975. Immensely successful in her new home, she is shown here making her only call at Tobermory, on 16 April 1987, on a special sailing in conjunction with the Mull Music Festival.

Caledonia (1970)
On 27 May 1977 she was chartered by the Design Council to carry a special party to view an oil rig under construction at Kishorn. She is seen arriving back at Kyle of Lochalsh with the party, with *Lochalsh* crossing her stern.

Skye Ferry, 1960s style
In the post-war years the Kyle–Kyleakin ferry was operated by the Caledonian Steam Packet Co. using a variety of small vessels. In the photograph taken on 24 July 1969, we see *Portree* on the left and *Coruisk* on the right. Both would eventually end up on the Clyde, *Portree* at Colintraive and *Coruisk* at Largs, although the latter did return to the islands as a relief vessel. (Lawrence Macduff)

Coruisk (1969)
Coruisk was introduced on the Kyle–Kyleakin service in 1969 but was rendered unemployed upon the delivery of *Kyleakin* and *Lochalsh*. Converted to bow loading, she was transferred to the newly established Largs–Cumbrae Slip service in 1972 but the traffic levels soon became too much for her. Replaced by *Isle of Cumbrae* in 1977, she became a spare vessel in the fleet and is photographed alongside the redundant Clyde car ferry *Cowal* at Greenock.

Lochalsh (1971) and *Kyleakin* (1970)
The Skye flotilla on 21 June 1987. *Lochalsh* is at the moorings off Kyleakin while *Kyleakin* is coming into the Kyleakin slipway. Within ten years of their introduction, both vessels were incapable of dealing with the volume of traffic on the route.

Kilbrannan (1972)
In 1972 the first of the eight Island class of small landing craft-type ferries entered service. Named *Kilbrannan*, she appropriately started a new service across Kilbrannan Sound from Lochranza on Arran to Claonaig in Kintyre. As this was a summer-only service, she was available for relieving work during the winter and in October 1972 she was chartered by Western Ferries to relieve on their Port Askaig–Feolin (Jura) service. She is seen at Feolin on 31 October. Note the CSP house flag and yellow funnel – the only one to have this livery.

Kilbrannan
After having spent her early years on the Clyde, latterly as one of the Largs–Cumbrae Slip 'flotilla', *Kilbrannan* was transferred to the Outer Hebrides in May 1977 to take over the Scalpay–Kyles Scalpay ferry service. She is photographed that year using the temporary slipway at Scalpay beside the new slipway that was being constructed to accommodate her. Note the rather tight fit!

Morvern (1973)
The second of the Island class ferries to be delivered was named *Morvern*, rather appropriately as she was to open the new service linking Lochaline in Morvern with Fishnish on Mull. She duly entered service on 1 May 1973 and is shown here at Lochaline. Note the MacBrayne white mast. It is rather sobering to compare her with the present incumbent of the route, *Loch Fyne*, as witness to the growth of traffic on the route.

Morvern
The old and the new off Iona. In 1979 the Fionnphort–Iona service became a car ferry service, with *Morvern* being the vessel so employed. She is seen passing behind the former ferry *Craignure*, which in August of that year was sold to Gordon Grant of Iona for livestock ferrying.

Bruernish (1973)
After *Morvern* came *Bruernish*, also in 1973. She replaced *Morvern* on the Fishnish crossing but was in turn superseded as more of the class came into service. Thereafter, she was used extensively throughout the network. All of the class were overhauled on the Clyde and sailed to and from there via the Crinan Canal. She is seen arriving at Crinan inward bound on 29 June 1976.

Bruernish
Known affectionately as the 'Daft Ducks', the Island class became ubiquitous on the West Coast
and would go anywhere they were able to land on a beach or slipway. On 17 May 1978, she
made several visits to Inverie on Loch Nevis with builders' vehicles from Mallaig. She is shown
landing her vehicles on the beach at Inverie.

Rhum (1973)
When delivered in June 1973, *Rhum* replaced *Kilbrannan* on the Lochranza–Claonaig service.
As this was a seasonal service she was available for relief work during the winter and is seen
lying at Kyleakin on 16 March 1974 while acting as spare to cover the overhauls of *Kyleakin*
and *Lochalsh*.

Rhum

Many and varied were the places visited and the duties undertaken by the Ducks, but perhaps one of the most unusual occurred in September 1988, when *Rhum* was chartered to transport rock from Ailsa Craig to Girvan. She is shown at Paddy's Milestone loading her cargo.

Rhum

In October 1978 *Rhum* spent several days carrying out maintenance work on the buoys in West Loch Tarbert and laying some permanent moorings at Kennacraig. For several days she lay off service at the old Islay berth at West Loch Tarbert pier, where she is pictured.

Coll (1973)
In early 1977 *Coll* was chartered by Howard Doris to provide a service for workers from Kyleakin to an oil rig under construction in Loch Carron. To provide additional passenger accommodation, a Portakabin was welded to her car deck and she is seen in this condition at Kyle of Lochalsh. In the background is *Bute*, which was relieving on the Portree/Small Isles service.

Coll
In December 1973 the newly delivered *Coll* was allocated to the Fishnish–Lochaline service in place of *Bruernish*, which in turn had replaced *Morvern*! She is seen arriving at Lochaline in her original colours of all-white mast.

Pioneer (1974)
In 1974 Islay finally got a new vessel but not the one proposed in 1970. Instead, a new design of vessel modelled on the Clyde Juniper class was introduced. After a few years the traffic offering was too much for her and she was transferred to the Mallaig–Armadale crossing, for which a vehicle lift was installed. She also regularly relieved on the Small Isles run and is seen at Canna.

Pioneer
During her eventful career, *Pioneer* operated at some time on virtually every service provided by the company, with the exception of Stornoway. For several days in June 1981 she found herself on emergency sailings out of Oban in place of *Columba* and is here seen reversing into Coll on the 10th.

Suilven (1974)

After Clansman was introduced on the Stornoway–Ullapool service, it quickly became obvious that she could not cope with the traffic, particularly the large freight vehicles. CalMac then acquired a drive-through ferry that was under construction in Norway, and redesigned her to take over the route. Named Suilven, she entered service on 24 August 1974. She is seen alongside at Stornoway on 1 September.

Eigg (1975)

For most of her career Eigg has been closely thirled to the Oban–Lismore ferry service. However, especially in her early days, she found herself making special sailings and calls as required. She is shown at Eigg loading sheep on the beach. The photograph demonstrates the ability of the Ducks to land in the most inhospitable of places.

Eigg
On Sunday 1 October 1978 *Eigg* made her first ever visit to Muck to pick up a cargo of cattle. The manoeuvre to get her ramp down on to the tiny pier at Port Mor was particularly difficult and she had to lie off for several hours, awaiting the tide rising.

Eigg
On 3 October *Eigg* made several calls at Easdale to convey builders' vehicles to the island. On completion she then loaded some cattle and conveyed them to Oban. She is seen starting to load the livestock. In carrying the livestock she was following a custom dating back to the early days of David MacBrayne of providing special livestock sailings from a host of piers to Oban in the autumn.

Mallaig Lineup, 1995
In October 1995, while *Ulva*, the Eigg tender, was overhauling, *Eigg* operated a special service to the island of her name from Mallaig. She is seen arriving at the latter with *Lochmor* at the Small Isles berth, with *Iona* loading vehicles for Armadale.

Canna (1975)
When first delivered, *Canna* was used on a variety of routes but by 1977 had settled down to being the Fishnish–Lochaline ferry. By this juncture traffic on the route was growing rapidly, with the result that in the summer two vessels were required at peak times. She is seen leaving Fishnish with *Iona* in the background, inward bound to Oban.

Canna

On Sunday 29 April 1984, *Canna* was specially sent from Lochaline down the Sound of Mull to Tobermory to tender to *Columba*, which was on a special sailing from Oban for the Mull Music Festival. She is shown alongside at Tobermory, making ready to load the crowds for *Columba* anchored in the bay.

Raasay (1976)

Raasay was the last of the Ducks to be delivered to CalMac and entered service in April 1976 on temporary duty on the Largs–Cumbrae Slip service. She finally became a West Highland steamer in July of that year when she journeyed north to serve the island after which she was named. She is seen on 7 July, resting at Crinan pier after passage through the canal on her way north.

Raasay
When moving between the Clyde and Hebridean waters, the Ducks normally traversed the Crinan Canal rather than go round the Mull of Kintyre. *Raasay* is seen passing Cairnbaan on her delivery voyage in 1976, sailing in the wake of the *Linnet*.

Raasay
As no overnight crew accommodation was provided on the Ducks, they weren't allowed to sail day and night with only one crew onboard. Thus, when sailing from Clyde to Hebridean waters the journey had to be broken to tie up overnight while the crew slept ashore. *Raasay* is photographed berthed overnight at Isle Ornsay, Skye, while returning to Raasay from overhaul on the Clyde on 11 June 1977.

Isle of Cumbrae (1977)
To improve the service to Mull, the Lochaline leg was lopped off the service from Oban and replaced by a crossing to Fishnish in 1973. The traffic on the route grew so much that the Island-class vessels operating it could not cope and were replaced in 1986 by *Isle of Cumbrae*, seen here leaving Fishnish.

Claymore (1979)
Having damaged her bow at Castlebay and been sent to the Clyde for repairs, *Claymore* found herself pressed into service providing the annual Govan Shipbuilders' charter from Glasgow to Rothesay on Saturday 7 June 1986. She is photographed from the Erskine Bridge, sailing upriver the previous day to be in position for the sailing.

Claymore
From 1994 for several years, CalMac operated a weekend service from Ardrossan to Douglas in the Isle of Man, the first time a service had been operated to a destination outside Scottish waters. Sadly, the service was not a commercial success. *Claymore* is seen leaving Douglas.

Lochmor (1979)
Built to replace the *Loch Arkaig* on the Small Isles service, *Lochmor* brought a new standard of comfort and speed to the exposed route. She is berthed alongside the pier at Canna on 9 July 1983.

Lochmor
As well as sailing to the Small Isles and Armadale and performing cruises, *Lochmor* was sometimes employed on special duties. She is illustrated alongside a fish farm in Loch Kishorn on 2 October 1994 while on charter to the Salmon Growers' Association.

Isle of Arran (1984)
By 1994 *Isle of Arran* had become the Islay ferry in summer and a relief vessel in winter. On the latter duty she relieved her quasi-sister *Hebridean Isles* on the Uig–Tarbert and Lochmaddy service and is seen approaching Lochmaddy in November of that year.

Hebridean Isles (1985)
When *Hebridean Isles* was delivered to CalMac, she was unable to be employed on the Uig–Tarbert/Lochmaddy route for which she had been designed as the terminals weren't ready for her. Thus she was employed on reliefs and her first such duty was as Stornoway ferry. She is photographed passing Arnish Point at the Lewis port.

Hebridean Isles
While on the way from Tarbert to the Clyde for her annual overhaul in October 1994, *Hebridean Isles* briefly diverted to Armadale and Mallaig to carry out berthing trials in case she was ever required to operate the Mallaig–Armadale service. She is illustrated leaving Armadale on 30 October on completion of her successful trials.

Loch Striven (1986)
The first of the new Loch class was *Loch Striven* and she took up service on the Largs–Cumbrae Slip service on 4 July 1986. In August 1989 she found herself temporarily on the Fishnish–Lochaline service as part of a general post occasioned by the breakdown of the Skye ferry *Lochalsh*. She is seen arriving at Lochaline.

Loch Linnhe (1986)
Although primarily intended to partner *Loch Striven* on the Cumbrae Slip service, *Loch Linnhe* in her early days also found employment as the winter Fishnish–Lochaline vessel. She is shown at Lochaline on 11 February 1992.

Loch Riddon (1986)
In the mid-1980s CalMac ordered four new beach-loading ferries from builders at Hessle on the Humber for service on the Clyde and to the Islands. The third new vessel was *Loch Riddon* and she is seen here at Fort Augustus on 22 October 1986 while on her delivery voyage to the Clyde.

Loch Ranza (1987)
The last of the quartet that began with *Loch Striven*, *Loch Ranza* was intended to operate from her namesake to Claonaig. However, by 1992 the traffic offering had become too much for her and she was transferred to the Tayinloan–Gigha route. She is photographed at Gigha.

Isle of Mull (1988)
Although built to operate the important crossing from Oban to Craignure, *Isle of Mull* has also been used on other routes as required. In her early days she was utilised as the Stornoway vessel to replace *Suilven* and provide an increased passenger capacity for the Royal National Mod being held in Stornoway. She is photographed alongside at Stornoway in 1989.

Isle of Mull
In 1991, while relieving *Suilven* on the Stornoway service, *Isle of Mull* found herself uniquely sailing to Uig instead of Ullapool for several weeks, as the mainland linkspan was closed for maintenance. She was photographed leaving Uig on 27 October, en route to Stornoway.

Lord of the Isles (1989)
Lord of the Isles was built in 1989 to replace both *Columba* and *Claymore* on the services out of Oban. In the course of her working week she called at Tobermory, Coll, Tiree, Castlebay, Lochboisdale and Colonsay. In this shot she is seen approaching Castlebay with Kisimul Castle ahead of her.

Loch Fyne (1991)
In a bid to cope with the ever-increasing traffic on the Kyle–Kyleakin service, two large ferries were introduced in 1991. Both *Loch Fyne* and her sister *Loch Dunvegan* served the route until the Skye Bridge was opened in 1995. They were supposed to be sold but eventually were found other employment. The *Loch Fyne* is photographed leaving Kyle of Lochalsh.

Loch Dunvegan (1991)
Made redundant along with *Loch Fyne* on the opening of the Skye Bridge, both she and her sister *Loch Fyne* endured a long spell laid up before being found alternative employment. She is shown sailing from Lochaline to Fishnish while temporarily replacing her sister.

Loch Buie (1992)

To improve capacity on the busy Fionnphort–Iona crossing, a new vessel was ordered from Miller's yard at St Monan's in Fife. Named *Loch Buie*, she is pictured leaving the Caledonian Canal at Corpach on 23 June 1992 on her delivery voyage from the builders.

Loch Tarbert (1992)
Built to provide extra capacity on the busy Lochranza–Claonaig service, *Loch Tarbert* is seen at Fort Augustus on her way from her builder's yard at St Monan's to the Clyde on 19 July that year.

Isle of Lewis (1995)
By the early 1990s history had repeated itself at Stornoway when the ever-rising traffic became too much for the incumbent ferry and a larger vessel was required. Built on the Clyde, *Isle of Lewis* was the largest vessel built for the company and is seen at Stornoway on 30 July with her predecessor *Suilven* berthed along from her.

Hamish Stewart

Hamish Stewart.

Iona (1970)
Throughout her life with the company, *Iona* was the Dunoon ferry, Stornoway ferry, Outer Isles ferry, Islay ferry and Armadale ferry. In addition, she relieved on most of the routes operated by CalMac. She is seen arriving at Oban while on relief duties.

Iona
In February 1979, *Iona* was at last able to take up service on the route for which she had been designed, that to Islay. She increased capacity on the route while for the first time offering passengers the chance to sleep on board overnight. Here she is seen turning round to reverse into Port Ellen.

Kyleakin
Before the advent of the bridge the main access for vehicles to sky was via the Kyle–Kyleakin ferry. To cope with the ever-increasing traffic, larger ferries were regularly introduced. Here we see *Kyleakin* of 1971 loading up at Kyleakin.

Lochalsh
Built at the same time as *Kyleakin*, *Lochalsh* could be identified by her different mast arrangement. She is also seen at Kyleakin. Both vessels were sold to Irish owners when replaced by *Loch Dunvegan* and *Loch Fyne* in 1991. Note Castle Moil in the background.

Bruernish
From their introduction until the 2000s, the Island class vessels were regularly given their annual overhaul at the Timbacraft yard at Shandon, which was situated in the shadow of the Clyde submarine base at Faslane. Here, a rather battered *Bruernish* can be seen lying at the yard in the company of one of her sisters.

Rhum

On Monday 17 March *Rhum* became the last vessel to be employed on the Scalpay–Kyles Scalpay route. In this photograph she is seen arriving at Kyles Scalpay. In the background can be seen the new Scalpay bridge. The new structure opened to great fanfare at 11.00 on Tuesday 16 December 1997. At 11.15 *Rhum* gave the last sailing from Kyles Scalpay, thus closing a route which had opened in 1964.

Pioneer

In 1989 *Pioneer* was replaced at Mallaig by *Iona* and became fleet spare vessel. Her lift was removed and she was fitted with side ramps to enable her to call at both Dunoon and Rothesay. As spare vessel she was employed with *Iona* in relieving *Isle of Arran* at Brodick in 1991 and is seen here leaving Ardrossan on a back-up sailing to the larger vessel.

Coll

In 1996 *Coll* became the Oban–Lismore ferry and stayed as such until Tuesday 16 December 1997. By then, with the introduction of new tonnage into the fleet, she was effectively redundant and was eventually sold in April 1998, along with her sister *Rhum*, for further service in Ireland. She is seen here at Lismore.

Eigg
In the summers of 1997 and 1998, *Eigg* was utilised on the Tobermory–Kilchoan service. The main reason for this was that, as she was only member of her class to have a Class IIA certificate, it made sense to have her near the Small Isles in case of emergencies. In this photograph she is seen alongside at Tobermory.

Eigg
New MCA regulations were introduced in 1999 and insisted that a helmsman in the wheelhouse had to have a clear, unrestricted view forward. As large vehicles often impeded the view on an Island class vessel, it was decided that *Eigg* should become the dedicated Lismore vessel and have the wheelhouse raised. In August of that year the black paint on the hull was also raised to the top of the car deck.

Isle of Cumbrae
After spending time operating on the Cumbrae Slip, Fishnish–Lochaline and Colintraive–Rhubodach services, *Isle of Cumbrae* became the summer Tarbert–Portavadie vessel in 1999. She is seen here leaving Tarbert. In winter she is mostly spare although she has relieved at Largs and Colintraive.

Raasay

In 1997 the delivery of *Loch Alainn* allowed a vessel cascade to take place which ultimately saw *Loch Striven* take over the Raasay service. Thus displaced after twenty years' yeoman service, *Raasay* became spare vessel at Oban although she did take over the Tobermory–Kilchoan service in winter. One regular duty was to relieve *Eigg* on the Lismore service and she is seen leaving Oban bound for that island.

Raasay

From almost her delivery in 1976 until 1997, *Raasay* was the dedicated ferry to the island after which she was named. This involved sailing from the new slipway beside the old pier at Suisnish over to the Skye terminal at Sconser. In this photograph she is seen unloading traffic at the Raasay side.

Claymore (1979)
Upon the delivery of *Lord of the Isles* in 1989, *Claymore* was transferred from the Oban-based services to replace *Iona* on the Islay service while the latter went to Mallaig. However, between 20 July and 19 August they switched as *Iona*'s hoist was out of action. Here, she is seen arriving at Mallaig.

Claymore
Between 1989 and 1993, *Claymore* operated very successfully between Kennacraig and Islay, her accommodation being superior to that of her predecessor, *Iona*. In this photograph she is making her way down the West Loch en route to Islay.

Lochmor (1979)
By 2000 the faithful *Lochmor* was coming to the end of her career on the Small Isles route. However, as her replacement, *Lochnevis*, would not be ready for the summer season the older vessel had to be overhauled to renew her passenger certificate. She is seen off Renfrew on Saturday 18 March, about to return north to Mallaig.

Isle of Arran
After serving the island of her name for nine years, *Isle of Arran* was transferred to the Islay route in 1993 and is seen coming alongside at Port Askaig. Subsequently she has served as fleet spare vessel and in 2013 returned to the haunts of her youth to partner *Caledonian Isles* on the summer Arran service; this also included a new service from Ardrossan to Campbeltown.

Isle of Arran
Having been replaced at Islay by *Hebridean Isles* in 2002, *Isle of Arran* spent July and August of that year operating additional sailings out of Oban to supplement those carried out by *Clansman*. She is seen arriving at Oban in August as *Clansman* was leaving.

Hebridean Isles
In May 1986, drive-through operation arrived on the Uig services in the shape of *Hebridean Isles*. In this photograph she is turning round to leave from Tarbert (Harris). Replaced by the much larger *Hebrides* in 2001, she has since forged a successful career on the Islay service.

Hebridean Isles
Hebridean Isles is pictured arriving at Lochmaddy in July 1996. When introduced into service, her hull painting, with the zigzag between black and white, was unique, but it was eventually emulated on *Isle of Arran*.

Loch Striven
Loch Striven and *Loch Linnhe* entered service on the Cumbrae Slip service in 1986. However, the delivery of *Loch Alainn* in 1997 allowed *Loch Striven* to be transferred to the Western Isles to become the Sconser–Raasay ferry. She served on this route with distinction until being replaced by the revolutionary hybrid vessel *Hallaig* in 2013. *Loch Striven* is shown arriving at Sconser.

Loch Linnhe
After a short spell operating on the Tarbert–Portavadie service, *Loch Linnhe* was transferred in 1999 to the Tobermory–Kilchoan service. With her large capacity, she offered the Ardnamurchan area its best ever ferry service. In winter she carries out general relief work at Raasay and Gigha, and has also visited the Sound of Barra. She is seen leaving Kilchoan bound for Tobermory.

Loch Riddon
Although primarily a Clyde vessel, spending the summer as second Cumbrae Slip ferry and part of the winter on the Tarbert–Portavadie crossing, *Loch Riddon* is also used for relief purposes in the Western Isles, principally at Iona and Gigha. She is pictured in the latter role, arriving at Oban.

Loch Ranza

In her early days, *Loch Ranza* operated the service across the Kilbrannan Sound from Lochranza to Claonaig in Kintyre. As this was a seasonal service, she was employed in general relief work in the winter. In this view she is approaching Largs while relieving on the Cumbrae Slip service on a glorious day in February 1991.

Isle of Mull and *Clansman* (1998)

In a typical summer scene in Oban Bay, *Isle of Mull* is on her way out of Oban bound for Craignure while *Clansman* is arriving from the Islands. Until the completion of the second linkspan at Oban, one vessel running late could lead to another having to lie off, waiting for the berth to become free.

Isle of Mull
Isle of Mull has faithfully served the island after which she is named since 1988. She is seen here sailing through the tidal race off the south end of Lismore. Even on a calm summer's day, this area can throw up an 'interesting' motion!

Lord of the Isles
Built to operate from Oban to Coll, Tiree, Castlebay and Lochboisdale, *Lord of the Isles* also operated the Mallaig–Armadale service between 1998 and 2002. She has also been used on the Islay route and acted as relief on the Craignure and Brodick services. She is seen arriving at Oban in July 1997.

Lord of the Isles
A rather worn *Lord of the Isles* is seen here arriving in Oban in January 1998. At the North Pier can be seen the former Skye ferry *Loch Dunvegan*. Newly overhauled after a lengthy lay up, she was on her way to Lochaline to replace *Isle of Cumbrae* on the Fishnish crossing. Ultimately, however, she was destined to be the Kyles of Bute ferry at Colintraive.

Loch Dunvegan
After a spell of lay up and attempts to sell her after the Skye Bridge opened in 1995, *Loch Dunvegan* returned to CalMac service as a spare vessel in 1997. However, from Wednesday 31 March 1999 she became the dedicated Colintraive–Rhubodach ferry and has remained there ever since, apart from relieving *Loch Fyne* at Lochaline. She is seen at Rhubodach.

Loch Fyne
In company with her sister *Loch Dunvegan*, *Loch Fyne* was returned to active service in 1997. In *Loch Fyne*'s case this was on the Fishnish–Lochaline service, where her large capacity proved a boon on this rapidly expanding route. She is seen leaving Lochaline still with white masts; these were repainted yellow in 1999.

Loch Fyne
As well as sailing from Lochaline to Fishnish, *Loch Fyne* has been called upon on several occasions to provide cargo runs to other destinations as required. Thus, she has been seen at Lismore and Corpach while so engaged. She is seen at Lismore where she has called on several occasions, the first being on Tuesday 13 February 2001.

Loch Buie
To deal with the large numbers of tourists visiting the holy isle of Iona, *Loch Buie* was introduced in 1992. Her design was adapted from that of *Loch Striven* but with an additional saloon over the car deck. She has been completely thirled to the route but did operate as second vessel on the Cumbrae Slip service during the Glasgow autumn holiday in 1997. She is seen leaving Fionnphort.

Loch Tarbert
Built in 1992 to serve between Lochranza and Claonaig, *Loch Tarbert* has also relieved at Portavadie and on the Sound of Barra and Sound of Harris services. She is seen leaving Oban, with *Lord of the Isles* at the North Pier.

Isle of Lewis (1995)
As the traffic on the Ullapool–Stornoway route travelled ever upwards, a new vessel was required in the 1990s to replace *Suilven*. Her replacement, *Isle of Lewis*, entered service in 1995 and was the largest vessel employed by the company. She is seen passing Rubha Airnis lighthouse at Stornoway.

Loch Bhrusda (1996)
In 1996 a new service was introduced across the Sound of Harris from Otternish in North Uist to Leverburgh in Harris. This new service allowed *Hebridean Isles* to concentrate on Uig–Lochmaddy and Uig–Tarbert sailings to cope with the ever-increasing traffic. *Loch Bhrusda* is shown here at Eriskay in August 2004. Due to the treacherous nature of the Sound, she was fitted with Schottel Pump Jet propulsion instead of the more usual Voith Schneider.

Loch Alainn (1997)
Although built for the Fishnish–Lochaline service, *Loch Alainn* spent very little time there and instead has worked the Colintraive–Rhubodach, Largs–Cumbrae Slip and Ard Mhor–Eriskay services, all very successfully. She is photographed leaving Rhubodach.

Loch Bhrusda
Loch Bhrusda soon became a victim of her own success and was replaced in 2003 by the larger
Loch Portain. She was then transferred to the new Ard Mhor–Eriskay service across the Sound
of Barra. With its introduction, the new service meant that the Outer Isles were joined by ferry
and causeway for the first time. She is seen on 6 August 2004 at Ard Mhor.

Clansman (1998)
The third *Clansman* joined the fleet in 1998 and was a replacement for *Lord of the Isles* on the Oban–Coll and Tiree and Oban–Castlebay and Lochboisdale services. Her fast speed and robust build made her instantly popular on both routes. She is seen leaving Oban on a misty morning in July 2001.

Clansman
In this view, *Clansman* is leaving Castlebay on a beautiful day. As well as her own routes, she has served as the fleet relief vessel and this has seen her sail on the Arran, Lochmaddy/Tarbert/Uig, and Stornoway routes as required.

Unusual Duo at Port Askaig
In March 1999, for the first time, *Lord of the Isles* was utilised on the Islay station, relieving *Isle of Arran*. At the same time, *Bruernish* was chartered by Serco to relieve their *Eilean Dhiura* on the Port Askaig–Jura service. Here the Lord is alongside at Port Askaig while *Bruernish* crosses from Feolin.

Oban, New Year 2000
All CalMac ships are in port on New Year's Day and here we see five vessels at Oban: *Eigg* and
Raasay nearest the camera, with *Isle of Mull* and *Clansman* at the Railway Pier while *Lord of
the Isles* nestles at the North Pier.

Lochnevis (2000)
Built as a replacement to *Lochmor*, this unique vessel brought the car ferry revolution to the Small Isles. Slipways were specially built at Rum, Eigg, Muck and Canna and her long stern ramp was designed to allow her to unload at them without actually grounding. She has also visited Castlebay on several occasions. In this photograph she is leaving Mallaig.

Lochevis and *Lochmor*
The old and the new photographed at Mallaig in November 2000. The new *Lochnevis* is alongside the linkspan for crew familiarisation trials while *Lochmor* leaves en route for the Small Isles. The new vessel entered service on Monday 20 November while the latter made her last CalMac voyage on Tuesday 5 December.

Laig Bay (2000)
Because of the deteriorating condition of *Ulva*, a new ferryboat had to be built to serve as tender at Eigg. The end result was *Laig Bay*, which took up station on Friday 22 December 2000. Her career with the company was short, as a new slipway that allowed *Lochnevis* to unload directly at the island came into use in 2004. To her fell the distinction of being the last small passenger ferry to be employed by the company. (Gordon Law)

Hebrides (2001)
Such was the success of the *Clansman* design, it was repeated for the new vessel built in 2001 for the Uig–Tarbert/Lochmaddy routes. Named *Hebrides* and launched by HM the Queen, the new vessel was fitted out to a high standard and proved instantly popular. In 2012/13, she emulated her quasi-sister by being fleet relief and she also found her way to the Oban services, Arran and Stornoway. She is seen on the Clyde with Blairmore Pier in the background.

Hascosay (1971)
To operate an overnight freight service between Stornoway and Ullapool, this much-travelled vessel was chartered from partner company Northlink for the summer of 2002. She entered service across the Minch on Wednesday 8 May and continued as such until Friday 27 September, when she transferred to her owner's Orkney and Shetland services. In her brief period at Stornoway she proved very popular.

Muirneag (1979)

Chartered from Harrison's (Clyde), this vessel took over the overnight Stornoway–Ullapool freight service on Saturday 28 September 2002 and operated as such until September 2013. Her funnels were painted in CalMac colours although initially the lions were the wrong way round! She experienced problems in coping with the Minch weather, which marred her efficiency somewhat.

Loch Portain (2003)
Loch Bhrusda's successor on the Sound of Harris crossing took up station on Thursday 5 June 2003. With a capacity of thirty-two cars she greatly increased the route's available space and became an instant success. She is seen here at Fishnish on Saturday 31 May 2003, undergoing ramp trials.

Coruisk (2003)
A vessel of unusual but imposing design, *Coruisk* entered service in 2003. She was designed to serve between Mallaig and Armadale in summer and in the Upper Firth of Clyde in winter, and could be manned by a relatively small crew. Her first year in service presented the company with many problems but she has since become a most efficient member of the fleet. She is seen leaving Armadale.

Coruisk
As well as the Skye service, *Coruisk* has also served on the Gourock–Dunoon and Wemyss Bay–Rothesay services. When not in service she has lain in the King George V Dock in Glasgow, the James Watt Dock in Greenock and alongside at Rosneath and Troon. She is seen arriving at Mallaig, with Skye as the backdrop.

Ulva (1956)
Although a minor member of the fleet, *Ulva* managed to record forty-four years' service and was the last of the red boats. In her early days she was employed at Iona and on reliefs but, in 1981, she was transferred to be the ferry at Eigg, tendering to *Loch Arkaig* and then *Lochmor*. By 2000 her hull was beyond economic repair and she was withdrawn. She is seen beached at Tobermory, awaiting disposal.

Hebridean Princess
Rendered unemployed by the arrival of *Lord of the Isles* in 1989, *Columba* was sold to a Yorkshire company who transformed her into a luxury cruise liner and renamed her *Hebridean Princess*. In her new life she has cruised the Western Isles, ranged as far as Ireland and Norway and has been chartered by the royal family. She is shown off Port Ellen. Her original crew would be astounded at the transformation!

THE WEST HIGHLAND STEAMER CLUB

The West Highland Steamer Club was founded in 1967 as an enthusiast group for those interested in the ships and services of David MacBrayne Ltd. Today, its main focus is on the ships and services of Caledonian MacBrayne in the Western Isles of Scotland.

MV Loch Ranza (1987)

THE CLUBS OBJECTIVES ARE . . .

- To maintain an interest in the vessels and operations of Caledonian MacBrayne and their predecessors, serving the West Coast and Western Isles of Scotland.
- To offer members the opportunity of meeting and sailing in a social and friendly atmosphere.

CLUB MEETINGS

The Club meets monthly during the winter months in Renfield St Stephen's Church Centre, Bath Street, Glasgow – 5 minutes walk from Charing Cross Station. Presentations are normally illustrated and speakers cover a wide variety of topics associated with West Highland Steamers and services.

MEMBERSHIP

The annual subscription entitles members to the full facilities of the Club, including copies of the illustrated Journal which is produced twice yearly around April and October. Members may also purchase photographs published in the Journal.

Nominated excursions on board Caledonian MacBrayne vessels are organised for the benefit of Club members. From time to time, other visits are arranged to ships and locations of interest to members.

CALENDAR

Each year the Club publishes a calendar for sale, illustrated with photographs of Hebridean vessels. It contains a mixture of modern and historic illustrations and is normally available by October each year.

www.westhighlandsteamerclub.co.uk

MV Isle of Lewis (1995)

MEMBERSHIP APPLICATION FORM

Name ....

Address ....

Postcode ....

Telephone ....

Email ....

Introductory membership fee £10

Make cheques payable to
West Highland Steamer Club

Signature ....

Date ....

Send completed application forms and membership fee to:

Robin Love, 29 Cyprus Avenue,
Elderslie, Renfrewshire PA5 9NB

Acknowledgements

The West Highland Steamer Club would like to thank the following for their help in the production of this book: Derek Crawford for writing the text and researching and writing the captions; Robin Love, Gordon Law and Lawrence Macduff for providing extra photographs; John Newth for digitising Hamish Stewart's photographs; Ian McCrorie for supplying the Jim Aikman Smith prints for selection; Gordon Law, Ian Somerville and Robin Love for choosing Jim Aikman Smith's photographs for inclusion; Murray and Myra Stewart for supplying and giving permission to use photographs from Hamish Stewart's collection and the National Records of Scotland for allowing the reproduction of prints from their collection Ref. GD469. We would also like to thank the staff at Amberley Publishing for their help and assistance.